Let’s Go!

Also by Lloyd Corder:

The Snapshot Survey
Quick, Affordable Marketing Research for Every Organization

Practical PR
How to Create Focused, Research-Based Campaigns that Produce Measurable Results

Leadership Communications
Achieving Outstanding Results in Today's Marketplace

Marketing ROI
Measuring & Maximizing Campaign Results

Marketing Research Management
A Step-by-Step Guide to Successfully Running Your Own Survey

The Marketing & Sales Cookbook
12 Recipes for Attracting & Retaining Great Customers

Stop Bellyaching!
It's Only a Presentation!

Let's Go!

Finding Your Way in Times of Exceptional Challenge

Lloyd Corder, Ph.D.

CorCom, Inc.
Research & Consulting

CorCom, Inc.
Gateway Towers, Suite 240
320 Ft. Duquesne Blvd.
Pittsburgh, PA 15222 USA
Tel: 412.201.2636 Fax: 412.201.2606
www.corcom-inc.com

Printed in the United States of America.

ISBN-10: 146-3692-390
ISBN-13: 978-14636-92391

First Edition

Copyediting and proofreading by Brittany Reno and Marianne Goldstein
Interior design and cover design by Brittany Reno.

CorCom, Inc. books are printed on long-lasting acid-free paper. When it is available, we choose paper that has been manufactured by environmentally responsible processes. These may include using trees from sustainable forests, incorporating recycled paper, minimizing chlorine in bleaching or recycling the energy produced at the paper mill.

This book is dedicated to everyone who has ever faced a daunting challenge and found the courage to overcome it.

Contents

Introduction

Let's Go! Is a Rallying Cry

There's a Time for Planning;
There's also a Time for Doing

I. William Goldfarb, M.D., walked up to the smart board and wrote, "Let's Go!" As part of a consulting assignment, I was in the middle of a sales and marketing strategy session talking about how to better communicate product offerings, refine the prospecting process, improve sales calls and close more business. A lot of ideas were being bantered about, but Dr. Goldfarb crystallized what we most needed to do with those two words.

We had talked and planned enough. It was now time to get moving and start getting results.

"Let's Go!" soon became our mantra in every meeting and conversation. We did not need the perfect plan or answers to every challenge; we just needed to stay focused on what we were trying to do and always make sure we were moving forward.

"Let's Go!" is the attitude you need to get through difficult and challenging periods. A plan is helpful, but without deliberate daily action, you can quickly fall into the trap of "perpetually getting ready." More preparation becomes a waste of time. It is time to move things forward.

It really does not matter how your crisis came to be—a bad economy, the latest bubble bursting, an unforeseen competitor innovation, a surprise downsizing, losing a major customer, personal stupidity or any other change that causes upheaval.

What matters is that you are—or may find yourself—smack dab in the middle of it. And the most important thing you need to do now is lead yourself and your troops through this mess to a better place.

When there is a meltdown, the people who are left get paralyzed. They hunker down. They stumble around for a direction. They let their fears get the best of them. They stop moving. It is up to you to get things going again.

This book is a compilation of quotes from my seminars, publications, consulting, teaching and research. They are organized into six categories, each representing a concept for each of the letters in the words Let's Go!

I thank those who have taken the time to tell me how these ideas have increased their productivity, boosted their inspiration and improved the quality of their lives—especially during times of great turmoil.

Whether you are the senior leader searching for a new direction, a mid-level manager who is in the midst of poor morale or a professional trying to make a positive difference, these ideas can help.

I offer them to you in the hope that they will aid you in this time of opportunity, help you chart a way forward and give you the courage to lead, so that one day, when you reminisce about this period, you see it as one of the most positive, defining moments of your career, company or personal life.

Let's Go!

There is already plenty of gloom,
depression and angst in the world.
Don't add to it.

Chapter 1

Lighten Up

Be an Unmistakable Optimist

Thinking positively breeds positive results—what you tell yourself on a daily basis will become a self-fulfilling prophecy.

If you are feeling like your life is out of balance, do things more efficiently or cut things out.

At the workplace, we come together as a team and should put our differences behind us.

Be pleasant, friendly and confident—there is nothing worse than interacting with someone who is rude. If you are friendly, you will have a much better chance of winning them over.

It is normal to feel uncomfortable. When we take action despite our fears, we expand our comfort zone. And, once expanded, we never fully revert back. The first step is the hardest.

Charisma, charm and personality may come more naturally to some than to others, but the skills of persuading others must be learned. People who learn to prioritize their family life become more productive at work. You feel less stress. When you are at work, you can focus on work. When you are at home, you can focus on home.

FOOTPRINT

If you realize that you are ultimately responsible for your achievements, you will accomplish more than if you blame others for your shortcomings.

Pray. Some of the most spiritual people I know own their own businesses. You need something to get you through the ups and downs.

Decide to make a good first impression. Research shows that it takes about four minutes for someone to decide whether they like you or not, how credible you are and how much they should trust you. The rest of the time, they will try to confirm or deny this first impression.

When presented with any opportunity, go with your gut instinct. An uneasy feeling about an assignment is a telltale sign that a job is not for you.

Send thank you notes. Everyone is sick of email, text messages and how impersonal our world has become. A handwritten note from your heart means a lot. I almost fell over when I saw that one of my customers had pinned to her wall a note that I had sent her. It was moving.

Smile. By smiling, you show that you are calm, confident and not fearful.

You can tell if a customer or prospect likes your product, service or idea by simply looking into his or her eyes. If they like what they are hearing, chances are that their pupils will be large. If not, their pupils will be smaller.

Think of something funny to say or an amusing story, if appropriate. The right humor can diffuse tense situations or even break the ice.

Admit when you are wrong or when you have made a mistake. It shows others that mistakes are okay, plus it builds trust. It is a lot better to act and make a mistake than sit back and do nothing.

Do not let your verbal (words) and nonverbal (actions, tone of voice, dress, etc.) signals contradict each other. People will always believe your nonverbal behavior, because it is harder to control and harder to lie about.

Get fired up! If you are excited and interesting, it will be easier for other people to listen to what you have to say.

If you want more success or meaning in your life, you need vivid, measurable goals that are based on passion. Because we are persuaded by what we see, when you make your goals visual, clear and specific, it is easier to see the path to their accomplishment.

Respect is greatly appreciated,

especially when people feel like their lives

are totally out of control.

Chapter 2

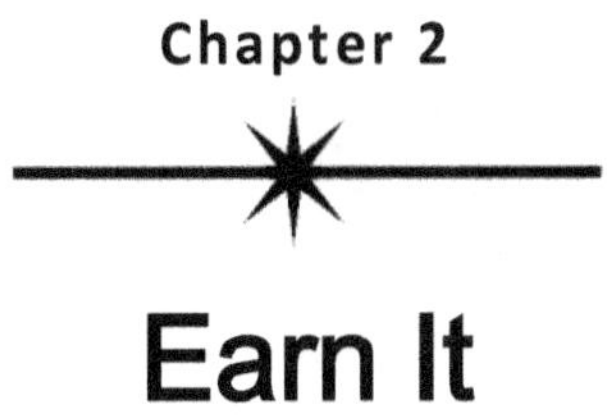

Earn It

Build Trust & Respect

Appreciate the law of reciprocity. You are only as good as what you give. "The hand that gives is the one that gathers."

People trust their friends', colleagues' or families' recommendations. A referral transfers that trust to you.

To really achieve your maximum potential, you need to find that person who will give you honest, constructive feedback instead of perpetual praise.

Be creative. Never directly come out and say that someone's opinion or idea is wrong. It is demoralizing. Instead, start off by saying, "I hear what you are saying, but my opinion differs a bit from yours. Do you mind if I expand?" By doing this, you are providing an alternative opinion.

Find advisors you trust, and listen to them. You cannot be an expert at everything. And you will not know if most of the advice your advisors give you is worth anything until some years later when you have to use it. Find good people and invest in those relationships.

Build relationships (not transactions) with customers. When a customer trusts you enough to help you solve an important issue in their business, you have a better relationship than if you are simply an order-taker.

Miscommunication is a major problem in our society and often wastes loads of time, money and effort. When both sides are clear on what the other wants and needs, the results will increase and improve dramatically.

When you frequently help others, they will often help you in return.

Your success is often linked with people you do not get along with. Not everybody has a good relationship with the members of their team, but in order to accomplish goals successfully there needs to be harmony within the group.

FOOTPRINT

Praise in front of a group. Discipline in private.

Growing a business and building relationships are one and the same. It is virtually impossible to do one without the other. Not only do we need strong relationships with people we already know, we need a way to continually transform strangers into prospects, then customers.

Disagree with an idea, but do not attack the person offering it. You can support the person, but not agree with his or her ideas.

Lifetime Customer Value (or the total amount that a customer invests in your business over the length of their relationship with you) is one of the most important marketing concepts you can use to grow your business. By its very definition, lifetime customer value forces us to focus on and build relationships with the customers we already have.

Stay in touch. It is so easy to get busy and communicate less and less... until there is little relationship left. Periodic updates, phone calls, notes, etc. help you maintain the important relationships that you have worked so hard to build.

No matter how much you dislike a person, remember that you are in a professional environment and have to keep your cool. Understand that if you stoop to their level, nothing positive will be accomplished. Make the effort to be civil.

Your mother was right: you are the company you keep. But the grade school adage extends far be-yond the playground and will follow you throughout your professional career. The people you surround yourself with can, and will, directly influence your success.

Resist partnerships unless you both contribute some-thing very unique and can stand to lose the other person as a friend. When one starts to think the other is not working or contributing enough, it can lead to problems—especially if you have strong personalities. Understanding these realities before you get in too deep can save a lot of heartache later.

Vow to learn as much as you can about your prospects and customers. Knowing why they buy (or decide not to buy) gives you the advantage.

FOOTPRINT

Saying "I" and "we" makes teamwork easier than saying "you."

Professional salespeople are not pushy and aggressive; they are persuasive, low key, service-oriented relationship-builders.

Periodic market research can be crucial to retaining customers and winning new ones.

Don't pull any punches.

Honest news is better than half-truths.

Chapter 3

Talk Straight

Tell the Truth

Master the art of saying "NO" to take control of your life. Saying no means learning to prioritize; it also means learning to communicate effectively. With established priorities and better communication skills, you become a more successful leader, boss, coworker, parent, spouse and friend.

The professionals know that asking questions is always more effective than making statements. When you ask a question, you get the other person thinking—and persuading—himself or herself.

People are persuaded by what they see.

Most marketing situations do not require highly precise marketplace feedback. Generally, someone does not need to know within a tenth of a percentage point how many people like or do not like a new product concept; they simply need to know if they are headed in the right direction. It is like coming to a stop sign: Go left, right or straight ahead, not three degrees to the north.

FOOTPRINT

Asking questions can have a magical power in influencing people to your point of view.

Help others sell your proposals and recommendations to their bosses. The easier you make it for them to accept your suggestions, the more work you will get.

If you are having any doubts, say no. People prefer to hear a positive mind change rather than a negative one.

When you are presenting, it is essential to have a main point or central theme. The rest of your speech is about supporting that idea with evidence, such as examples, testimony, statistics, graphics and analogies.

There is nothing more agonizing than the thought of having to face a hostile audience, so carefully package the order of your points. When you can, sandwich your most controversial idea in the middle of two or more positive points.

There are few things more frustrating than an unfocused, unproductive meeting. Problems include no agenda, inadequate preparation, starting late, ending late and not clearly defining who is going to do what by when.

Your options with a hostile audience are always simple. Face them head on, go for a compromise or run. However, winning in these situations is not so simple. You have to find a way to enable both parties to win.

If you do not have an answer, do not make something up or quote something inaccurately. This is exactly what your hostile audience wants you to do. It is better to get back to them with the correct information.

Do not talk about your customers behind their backs. Your attitude shows. Respect and value your customers—even when they are difficult to get along with or satisfy. If they are really that bad, stop working with them, but have the courage to give them the respect they deserve by holding them in high esteem.

"No" does not need to be harsh, nor does it need to compromise your work ethic. In fact, it should do the opposite. By saying "No" at the right time, you will be able to maximize your time and minimize failure.

When your employees believe in your vision, the purpose of your company, what you are trying to do for customers and everything else you are about, motivation gets easier. Without trust, the focus is on negativity and suspicions. Instead of asking themselves what they could be doing to delight your customers, employees are wondering if they are going to have a job.

Do not repeat negative or inflammatory language. Use your own words to answer a question and present your information. The words you say—even if they are not YOUR words—get quoted.

Creating an effective agenda is one of the most important elements for a productive meeting. The agenda communicates important information, such as topics for discussion, a presenter or discussion leader for each topic and time allotment for each topic. It provides an outline for the meeting.

Decide where you're going and

How you're going to get there.

Chapter 4

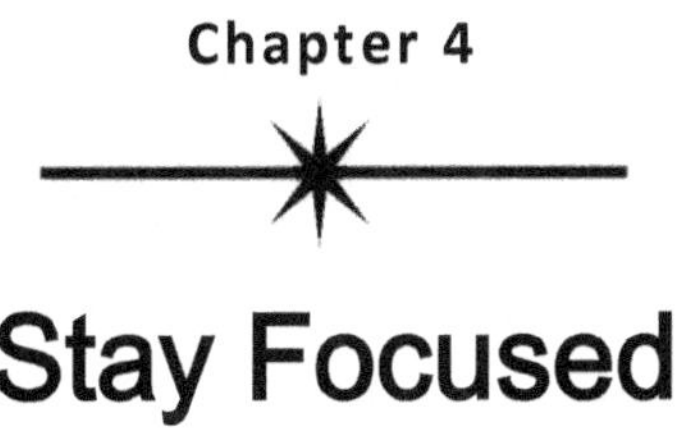

Stay Focused

Value Clarity

There is no doubt that clearly writing your business, product, marketing and personal goals can be the only thing that stands between accomplishing them and falling flat on your face. It is really that simple. Decide what you want, and write it down.

Remind yourself that it is better to have a few great projects completed than to have many average ones. You want to feel great about your work and know that you put all the time and effort into it that you possibly could.

To stay in business, you need to earn more than you spend, and the higher the ratio of revenue over investment, the more successful the business.

Focus on creating value—not doing activity. How long it takes you to do something is irrelevant. What you can get done in the time you have is the issue. By focusing on the broader objectives that your customers are trying to reach, you can help them with what is most important to their businesses.

FOOTPRINT

To admit shortcomings but not work toward betterment is simply foolish.

Prioritize tasks. Begin by making a to-do list and ranking tasks in order of importance. Be realistic and break down larger tasks into smaller ones so that they appear less daunting.

Beepers, timers and other machines that ring can be used to control the amount of time you give to a specific task. Set one for 30 or 60 minutes, then get busy working.

Taking on more tasks rarely equals greater chances for success. Instead, we drown in activities. Think of yourself like a sponge: If you soak up too much, you cannot do your job at all. Overflowing with activities, we struggle to do our best in any one thing, let alone succeed at everything. Getting something to "good enough" almost always beats "working on it until it is perfect."

Do it right the first time. As a manager, you do not want to spend all of your time "firefighting" or fixing problems. Do not be afraid to acknowledge problems that cause mistakes and correct them. Determine how to prevent reoccurring problems.

Delegate. Assign tasks to the appropriate people. Somebody who knows what he or she is doing will be able to complete the task more quickly with fewer mistakes. If possible, try to delegate tasks to individuals who enjoy those jobs.

Clarify and focus. When people do not understand the purpose of the job, they waste time. Make sure to clearly explain the procedure, purpose and significance of the job.

Avoid procrastination. People procrastinate either because they have a lack of information or fear of failure. If there is a lack of information, it is best to stop thinking about the problem and start looking for ways to solve it. With the appropriate amount of information available, the fear of failure can be alleviated.

Resist fixed expenses at all costs (additional employees, rent and other cost that show up every month—regardless of how much work you have or do not have)! The lower you can keep these, the easier it will be to weather tough economic times and the easier it will be for you to operate in agile and flexible ways.

Spending more time on more important tasks is key, rather than wasting time on mundane jobs. Be reasonable when deciding how much time to allot for a task. Rushing to finish on time, or having to delay other scheduled tasks because you did not plan enough time for the given job, will result in a jumbled schedule and lower quality work.

A business plan precisely defines your business, identifies your goals and serves as a basic guide for get-ting from where you are today to where you want to be in the future.

Focus both inside and outside your firm.

Don't hide in your office.

Chapter 5

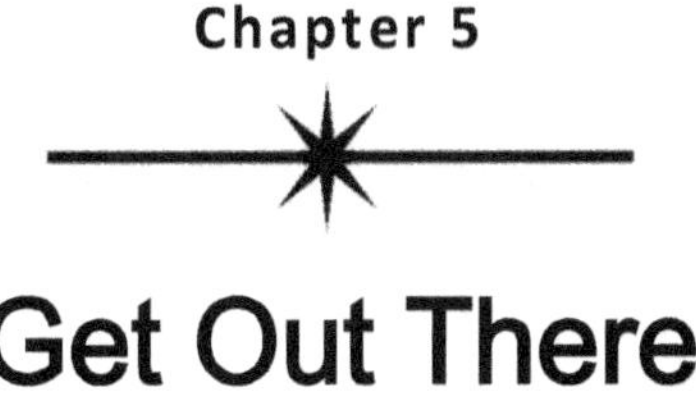

Get Out There

Be Highly Visible

Marketing and selling is a continual process and an ongoing effort for all companies.

If you are thinking about reducing or eliminating your marketing, IT, human resources or other functions because of the economy, PLEASE TAKE A DEEP BREATH. Do not do it! This may be your best chance to win market share, implement new systems or build your staff. As your competitors are slowing down, you can jump past them.

Learn how to sell, and find a way to get better at it. In professional services, customers are buying you. The more time you have—and the more effective you are—the more sales you will generate.

Big-time selling is typically the result of doing a lot of little things right. It involves the intangibles that go way beyond the questions you ask, the literature you use or the proposals you write.

Think of advertising, production, human resources and other functions as an "asset" for your business instead of an "expense" and drain on the budget.

Your website can be your company's best friend or worst enemy. If your website is aesthetically appealing and easy to use, your visitors will be much more inclined to purchase your products and services. On the other hand, if your website is difficult to read and looks unprofessional, it is unlikely that your visitors will be sold on choosing your company to invest their money.

It is important to get your name out there. Even though most companies do not have current news to report, they find new and creative ways to get the word out.

Email has made marketing both easier and more difficult. It is easier because, in a few seconds or minutes, you can send a lot of people low-cost communications. It is more difficult though, because people are sick and tired of being pestered to death with junk!

FOOTPRINT

Networking has been around for ages, though we just recently gave it a name. It used to be called helping!

Make "executive transience" part of your marketing strategy. This is when your customer leaves one company and goes to another. It is a great marketing tool and further demonstrates the value of helping people, especially your customers, with their job transitions, when you can.

Ask your customers and colleagues for advice. Customers always have great insights about your business. Many have already successfully addressed the problems you are currently facing.

Remember, you cannot magically increase the number of hours in a day. However, if you manage your time efficiently and effectively, you can make the most of the hours that you DO have. Done properly, time management will give you the illusion that you can magically create more hours.

Do not wait for your customers to volunteer information. Providing referrals is a learned behavior. You have to train your customers to think of you—and think of you frequently—to get referrals.

It is my contention that every business should require its employees to wear a uniform, even if the uniform is business casual dress or a three-piece suit; there should be a standard. Knowing and following the "unspoken" dress code can make all the difference in how easily and passionately others accept your ideas.

Everybody in your organization can play a role in selling, if you let them. By taking a deeper look at how you are answering the phone, writing your proposals or asking existing customers for referrals, there may be myriad opportunities to do more with what you already have.

It is okay to ask for what you want. Most people like to be helpful, as long as you are not pestering them too much or asking for something too ridiculous.

Stop pretending that you have all of the ideas and solutions. Ask others what they think.

Chapter 6

Open Up

Listen More

For every 10 books about selling, presentation and other "talking" skills, there is less than one book about listening. However, listening is one of the most important activities that we do day-in and day-out. The better listeners we are, the better results, more happiness and greater satisfaction we attract.

Listen carefully. Listening is the most important thing you do. You should avoid distractions like listening to music, playing computer games and looking out the window. You should listen to every word said. This will make the information you gather much more valuable.

When you listen intently, you hear the detailed thoughts and insights. You do not have to guess about what they mean. Just ask them what is important to them, then ask follow-up or probing questions to find out WHY they think the way they do.

You are unique, just like everybody else. Listen and look for natural connections and common interests.

Listening helps us understand how people talk about things in their own words, which may be very different from your preconceived notions.

Take notes. It aids your memory and flatters your listener.

When you are face-to-face, you can physically show something to participants, such as ad mock-ups, software or product demonstrations, TV commercials or new bill formats. You can see their nonverbal reaction and listen to their verbal response. It is the next best thing to being a fly on the wall.

Customers buy their words, not yours. Listen to the WORDS your prospects use to describe their current situation—then use those words in your written proposals, solutions and follow-up conversations. It will prove that you are listening, and it will help you build rapport and common ground.

Know when to solve a problem versus let someone vent. A lot of people just want someone to listen to them; they simply need to get something off their chests.

Being polite enhances listening.

Be completely focused on listening, not multitasking. Put away the Blackberry, look away from your computer screen and give your attention to the speaker. A few minutes of highly focused attention and feed-back is a lot better than pseudo-listening.

Focus on key points. Try not to get lost in the details but to center in on the big picture.

If people have to constantly repeat what they just said to you, you are not listening.

When you listen more than you talk, other people will appreciate this. We tend to like people who listen to us.

Beyond the words, listen for what is NOT being said. What someone leaves out speaks volumes about what they are really thinking or feeling.

Ask people what they want. What problem will it solve for them? What value does a solution bring? This approach helps you uncover underlying needs.

Make it easy for other people to listen to you. An easy way to do this is to put numbers in front of your points. When someone asks you a question, say, "There are three things you can do. First, ... Second, ... Third, ..."

Index

N

O

P

R

S

T

U

V

W

About the Author

Lloyd Corder, Ph.D., is founder and CEO of strategic marketing research firm CorCom, Inc. and teaches at Tepper School of Business at Carnegie Mellon University. He is a frequent keynote, convention and motivational speaker, and he has appeared on business-oriented radio and television programs. Corder's studies have been published in more than 500 magazines and newspapers.

Recent books, free resources and other helpful materials are available at CorCom, Inc.'s website or directly from the company. You can also order this and other printed books or Kindle downloads from Amazon (www.amazon.com).

CorCom, Inc.
Gateway Towers, Suite 240
320 Fort Duquesne Boulevard
Pittsburgh, Pennsylvania, 15222 USA

www.corcom-inc.com
info@corcom-inc.com
412.201.2636

www.ingramcontent.com/pod-product-compliance
Lightning Source LLC
Chambersburg PA
CBHW031230170526
45165CB00004B/1655
* 9 7 8 1 4 6 3 6 9 2 3 9 1 *